for lovers of dogs,
big and small.

MOLLY
the dog with diabetes

By Kevin Coolidge

Illustrated by
Stephanie "Stubby" Webb

Woof, my name is Molly and I'm a little dog with diabetes. Diabetes is an illness. Don't worry. I am healthy now. My friends love me. My family loves me. I love them. I am happy.

I can do everything dogs can do. I just needed to learn to take care of my health. My life has changed since my mommy and daddy found out I have diabetes. I need to do certain things to remain healthy and safe.

I have to eat every twelve hours, and I do love to eat! I have special dog food, and can't eat any "people food" anymore. It's ok, because my special food gives me everything I need.

I get two shots every day. My shots don't hurt. I am a good girl. I get a treat after each shot. I like milkbones. These shots provide what my body can't make anymore, insulin.

I visit the doctor for check-ups. This is to check my health and keeps me feeling well. Sometimes I am scared when I go to the vet, but the vet is a nice man. He loves animals and he helps keep me healthy and happy.

Every day I have a special routine. My daddy takes me outside to pee. I pee in a cup. My daddy uses a special strip to see what my blood sugar is so he knows how much Vetsulin goes into my shot that day. Vetsulin is a medicine for pets with diabetes.

It's time for breakfast! The special dog food helps keep my blood sugar in control. Morning is when I receive my first shot. It is important that I eat first so that the vetsulin can do its job. Diabetes can cause a problem where my blood sugar can get too high, or too low. This food and my routine help keep it balanced.

Sometimes my blood sugar goes too low and I feel tired and shaky. I have trouble walking and just want to sleep. When this happens, it's called hypoglycemia. My mommy gives me a couple licks of honey, and soon I feel like my doggy self.

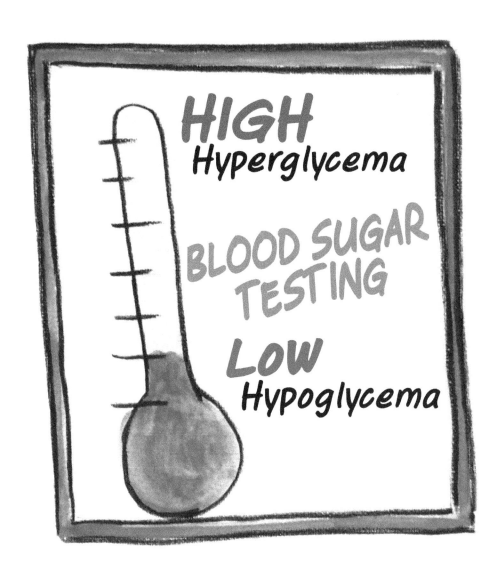

My mommy takes me for a walk every day because it is important for me to exercise so I don't gain too much weight. Being overweight makes my diabetes worse. I love my walks. I get to see what is happening in my neighborhood.

on my walk, I see squirrels and chipmunks. I see my neighbors and get nice ear scratches. I see the cat next door. I hear birds. I smell the deer that cross the road. I feel the warm sun on my fur. I love going for a walk.

During the day, I do doggy things. I play with my squeaky toy. I bark at the mailman. I take a nap. I play with my brother, Buck. We wait for our humans to come home.

Twelve hours after breakfast, I eat my supper, and I get my second shot of the day. I play fetch with Mommy. I play tug of war with Daddy. I watch TV and bark at the animals on TV. When it is time for bed, I jump on the big bed with Mommy and Daddy and go to sleep. It is a great doggy day.

My name is Molly and I'm a little dog with diabetes. Don't worry. I am healthy. My friends love me. My family loves me. I love them. I am happy, woof.

More About Molly

Molly is a seven year old daschund mix. Molly was born at an animal shelter and adopted by the Powers family, Sue and Fred. When she was four years old, Molly started acting strange. She was hungry and thirsty all the time. She started urinating on the kitchen floor, something she hadn't done since she was a little puppy.

Sue thought Molly might have a urinary tract infection, and took her to a local veterinarian, Dr. Rusty. The doctor examined Molly and used a needle to draw blood. After many tests, Dr. Rusty told the Powers that Molly had **diabetes**.

What is diabetes? Diabetes is a disease where your body's ability to produce or respond to the hormone insulin doesn't work correctly. To understand diabetes, you need to understand insulin. When you eat, your body turns food into sugars, known as **glucose**.

Your pancreas, an organ in your body, is supposed to release insulin. Insulin serves as a "key" to open your cells, to allow the glucose to enter, and allows you to use the glucose for energy. If you have diabetes, this system doesn't work correctly.

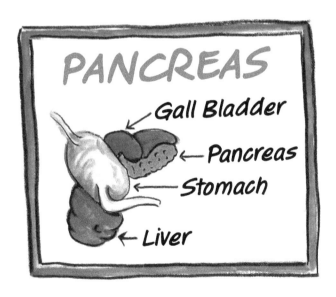

Your blood sugar can go too low and you can feel tired, shaky and confused. When this happens, it's called hypoglycemia. The first time it happened to Molly she had trouble walking and just wanted to sleep. Sue was worried. She thought Molly was dying, but Doctor Rusty told her to give Molly a couple licks of honey, and soon Molly was feeling good again.

Dogs, cats, humans and other animals can get diabetes. Your pet and you can still live a healthy, happy life, but you must take special care. Your local veterinarian is an important resource for the care of your pet, just like your doctor will teach you how to be healthy if you have diabetes.

Your veterinarian and helpers can teach you how to check your pet's blood sugar every day. They will show you to fix the shots with the right amount of dog insulin, which is called vetsulin. Your vet will teach you how to clean your dog's neck with alcohol, and how to give the injection without hurting your pet.

Exercise is important for all pets, but it's especially helpful for keeping your pet with diabetes healthy and happy. Being overweight will make diabetes harder to control. Your pet will still be able to do all the things that you love to do together. You just have to make sure to provide special care for them.

Dogs love to eat, and people love to share their food with their dogs. It's important to only give your dog the special food that the vet teaches you to feed them. It's also important to feed them at the correct times. Different dogs may have different routines. Be sure to follow your vet's directions.

Molly lives a full happy life. She has two children that come to visit her often, Reanna and Jacob. They take her on walks, play with her, and learn how to properly feed, care, and give her shots. They love Molly and Molly loves them.

Molly has two best doggy friends who often visit. Bella is a big black lab and Austin is a little Daschhund. Molly doesn't let diabetes stop her from having fun. Molly and her friend go on walks. They play with balls. They swim in ponds. They have fun.

Molly doesn't let diabetes keep her from going on vacation. Every fall, her mommy and daddy take her to the beach. She stays at a "pet friendly" hotel. She meets new friends, plays in the sand, and chases seagulls. She never seems to be able to catch them.

Molly is a little dog with a big heart. Yes, she has diabetes, but she is happy and healthy. Her friends and family love her, and she loves them. She does all the doggy things that dogs do, and she loves her life. If your dog has diabetes, your pet can be happy and healthy too!

About the Author

Kevin resides in Wellsboro, just a short hike from the Pennsylvania Grand Canyon. When he's not writing, you can find him at *From My Shelf Books & Gifts*, an independent bookstore he runs with his lovely wife, several helpful employees, and two friendly cats, Huck & Finn.

He's recently become an honorary member of the Cat Board, and when he's not scooping the litter box, or feeding Gypsy her tuna, he's writing more stories about the Totally Ninja Raccoons. Be sure to catch their next big adventure, *The Totally Ninja Raccoons Discover the Lost World*.

You can write him at:

From My Shelf Books & Gifts
7 East Ave, Suite 101
Wellsboro, PA 16901

www.wellsborobookstore.com

About the Illustrator

Stephanie "Stubby" Webb was born in Iowa in 1981. She's been studying art since she was three years old. Her interests include photograpy, music, gardening, and Ving Tsun (pronounced 'wing chung') Kung Fu. Her goal is to become a Sifu (teacher). She's an advocate for victims of abuse. She has two cats named Tilly and Orion. Check her out on Facebook on Genre of Stubby.

Kevin is also the creator of *The Totally Ninja Raccoons*. The books are about three raccoons who decide to become ninjas because they already have the masks. *The Totally Ninja Raccoons* is a series of early chapter books, targeting audiences first through fourth grade.

The books are short adventures with quick chapters, specially structured to encourage reluctant readers. Short chapters, humor, adventure, and one picture per chapter keep kids feeling a sense of engagement and accomplishment as they plow through these stories and ask for more!

Available at *From My Shelf Books & Gifts*
on the Internet at www.wellsborobookstore.com,
or wherever books are sold.

THE TOTALLY NINJA RACCOONS MEET BIGFOOT

by Kevin Coolidge

THE TOTALLY NINJA RACCOONS MEET THE WEIRD & WACKY WEREWOLF

by Kevin Coolidge

THE TOTALLY NINJA RACCOONS AND THE SECRET OF THE CANYON

by Kevin Coolidge

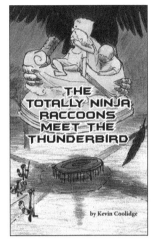

THE TOTALLY NINJA RACCOONS MEET THE THUNDERBIRD

by Kevin Coolidge

THE TOTALLY NINJA RACCOONS AND THE CATMAS CAPER

by Kevin Coolidge

THE TOTALLY NINJA RACCOONS AND THE SECRET OF NESSMUK LAKE

by Kevin Coolidge

THE TOTALLY NINJA RACCOONS MEET THE LITTLE GREEN MEN

by Kevin Coolidge

THE TOTALLY NINJA RACCOONS MEET THE JERSEY DEVIL

by Kevin Coolidge

Before Molly, before ninja raccoons, there was Hobo the Cat. Kevin's first book, *Hobo Finds A Home*, is a true story about a little kitten. Hobo the Cat leaves the farm, has big adventures, makes a new friend, and finds a forever home.

Hobo was the bookstore cat at *From My Shelf Books & Gifts* for many years. His many jobs included playing with children, delighting cat lovers, and soaking up sunshine to spread to everyone he met. This is his story...

Available at *From My Shelf Books & Gifts*
on the Internet at www.wellsborobookstore.com,
or wherever books are sold.

CPSIA information can be obtained
at www.ICGtesting.com
Printed in the USA
BVHW011156060119
537157BV00008B/455/P

9 781643 706771